Edward Foley

preaching basics

A MODEL AND A METHOD

LTP
LITURGY
TRAINING
PUBLICATIONS

Acknowledgments

This book has been, from the beginning, a collaboration. Among those whose conversation I have enjoyed or whose insights I have gratefully received are Richard Fragomeni, Patricia Parachini, Gail Ramshaw and Peter Rehwaldt. Their contributions, and those of others, have certainly enhanced this work.

Edward Foley

Excerpts from the English translation of *Lectionary for Mass* © 1969, 1981, International Committee on English in the Liturgy, Inc. (ICEL); excerpts from the English translation of *Eucharistic Prayers for Masses of Reconciliation* © 1975, ICEL; excerpts from the English translation of *Documents on the Liturgy, 1963–1979: Conciliar Papal, and Curial Texts* © 1982, ICEL. All rights reserved.

Excerpts from *Fulfilled in Your Hearing* © 1982, United States Catholic Conference, Inc., Washington, D.C. Used with permission. All rights reserved.

Copyright 1998, Archdiocese of Chicago: Liturgy Training Publications, 1800 North Hermitage Avenue, Chicago IL 60622-1101; 1-800-933-1800, fax 1-800-933-7094, e-mail orders@ltp.org.

This book was edited by Gabe Huck. Audrey Novak Riley and Bryan Cones were the production editors. The design is by Jill Smith and M. Urgo, and the typesetting was done by Kari Nicholls in Caslon and Officiana. Printed by RPP Printing Enterprises, Inc., in Libertyville, Illinois.

04 03 02 01 00 99 98   6 5 4 3 2 1

1-56854-170-8

PREACH

contents

Foreword

■ Preaching impacts, preaching disrupts, preaching quakes. It impacts minds toward the understanding of the Word, placing into the consciousness of the hearer the dangerous memory of Christ. It disrupts the status quo by the power of the Spirit, inviting fresh ways of just living. It quakes the religious imagination to dream dreams of the new creation, offering the heart persuasive metaphors of the gift.

Preaching is central to the life of the church. It is the passionate presence of the ancient conversation between divinity and humanity. When the Word is preached, the Spirit moves and God speaks once more in human accents.

If this is so, then preaching cannot be thoughtless. It demands a commitment of intelligence, of creativity and of vigor. Preaching takes preachers who want to work hard and hearers who are willing to grasp a two-edged sword. It engages the preacher and the assembly in an innovative act of language which finds different shapes in the life of the community.

For instance, preaching takes place at moments when the gospel is first heard by hungry souls. It happens when the scripture and tradition of the church are interpreted and explained in the cultures and circumstances of human life. Preaching is the incantation of God's wonderful works in the liturgical assembly. During retreats and spiritual gatherings of believers, preaching inspires heroic conversion and perseverance in holiness. In each circumstance, preaching is an engagement of persons in a message that makes a difference.

In recent years, books, articles, journals, graduate curricula and certificate programs have emphasized the importance of preaching as an ecclesial activity demanding excellence and preparation. These define the genres of preaching and outline the various skills and methods by which preachers can create the preaching event. To contribute to this surge of interest, the bishops of the United States published a document on liturgical preaching, *Fulfilled in Your Hearing*.

Focusing on the unique genre of the homily, the document outlines the significance of liturgical preaching in the life of the church. The homily is an act of faith that interprets scripture, liturgy, life and the aspirations of the assembly. It engages the assembly toward a surrender of praise, and leads to a grateful sacramental encounter with the gift offered in the liturgical activity. The document suggests ways for preachers to prepare, deliver and evaluate the homily, encouraging the involvement of some members of the community.

The goal of this book is to develop the model and methods of liturgical preaching outlined in *Fulfilled in Your Hearing*. Crafted in conversations and consultations, Ed Foley's presentation places at the center of the task the vitality of passion: a passion for the Word, for the liturgy, for the people of God. This passion is the necessary precondition for the preacher to appreciate the challenges and directives of this work.

The core of this essay, and that which will demand the engagement of both the head and the heart of the preacher, are the chapters which offer the model and the method for carrying through this challenging approach to homiletics. The approach is not for the feeble. It is a creative integration of liturgy, scripture, art, culture and common sense that demands time and commitment. The promise of the resourceful approach is increased insight into the liturgical activity of preaching and a more meaningful proclamation of the saving mystery of Christ's passover.

As a professor of liturgy and homiletics, I find this essay extremely practical. It demonstrates and further explains the insight of *Fulfilled in Your Hearing* that the homily is a liturgical activity. The method presented herein weaves together the best of homiletic theory and practical theology. Understanding and practicing preaching as a sacred conversation can change one's understanding of the homily, its preparation and ultimately the consciousness of the preacher who engages the liturgical assembly.

— Richard Fragomeni

Chapter One

A Matter of Passion

At its core, effective liturgical preaching is a matter of passion.

"Passion" often means a compelling feeling or desire. This is not quite what we mean to say about preaching. Our word "passion" developed from a Latin word that meant "enduring" and "suffering." In its origins, the English "passion" almost always had a theological meaning that was rooted in the suffering of Christ. The passion required for preaching has this life-giving and enduring commitment.

Passion for the Word of God   God's Word reverberates through the world, assails us in news accounts, erupts from lectionary pages in prophecy and gospel. The Word is not a limp string of pious sayings nor an orderly collection of rules for life. It is more like an unpredicted thunderstorm that disrupts our plans and brings commerce to a standstill. The prophet Isaiah asserts that this divine torrent saturating the earth will not return to God empty. The one who embraces the ministry of liturgical preaching delights in this untamed Word and in the possibility that one path the Word will take on its journey back to the Holy One is right through the preacher.

Passion for the liturgy   This preaching is not simply *in* the liturgy or *at* the liturgy. It *is* the liturgy. The preacher's passion for the liturgy translates into an authentic commitment to public worship as the font and summit of both ecclesial and personal life. This is where we

> *Isaiah*
>
> For as the rain and the snow come down
>   from heaven,
> and do not return there until they
>   have watered the earth,
> making it bring forth and sprout,
> giving seed to the sower and
>   bread to the eater,
> so shall my word be that goes out
>   from my mouth;
> it shall not return to me empty,
> but it shall accomplish that which I purpose,
> and succeed in the thing for which I sent it.
>
> *Isaiah 55:10–11 (NRSV)*

discover and rehearse our vocation in the church and commitment to the world. The whole of the liturgy informs our preaching and must be embraced wholeheartedly for the sake of such preaching.

Passion for the baptized assembly   This passion is not like a parent's concern for children nor a teacher's concern for students. Rather, true passion for the assembly recognizes and embraces them as bearers of the Word, celebrants of the liturgy and *the* critical determinant for preaching.

A passion for the assembly means believing deeply that the people who assemble Sunday after Sunday are not the object of our preaching. Rather, they are one of the subjects. "Subject"

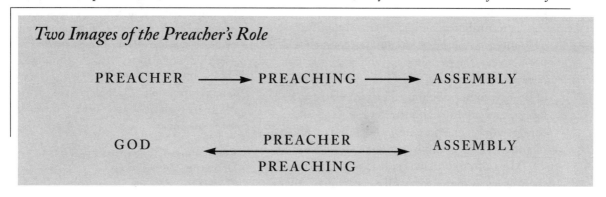

Two Images of the Preacher's Role

PREACHER ⟶ PREACHING ⟶ ASSEMBLY

GOD ⟵ PREACHER PREACHING ⟶ ASSEMBLY

here does not mean "subject of," much less "subject to." It means: When the verb is "preach," one subject is "assembly." For starters, their experiences and expectations are essential ingredients in the preaching event. This makes attentive listening a quality the preacher must ever cultivate.

The Turn toward the Assembly

A preacher's passion for the Word of God and for the liturgy are perhaps not surprising. What may be more challenging and transformative is a passion for the baptized assembly. This passion embraces the assembly as *doer* and not simply hearer in the preaching event. All that follows flows from this.

Liturgical preaching is an encounter. But who encounters whom? The essential encounter is not between the preacher and the assembly, but between the assembly and God! As in the whole of liturgy, so in preaching: The two who come face to face are God and the church, God and this assembly. The preacher, who is in fact also a member of the assembly, mediates this encounter.

Most often those who preach have imagined themselves as the subject of the preaching activity.

The assembly is imagined as the consumer or object of the preaching. But what if the assembly is intimately engaged, not as recipient, but as subject — a primary agent — of this preaching? Just as the *Constitution on the Sacred Liturgy* envisions the baptized as active subjects in the liturgy, so must they be subjects in the preaching that dares to call itself liturgical.

Fulfilled in Your Hearing: The Homily in the Sunday Assembly (FIYH) is a 1982 document of the United States bishops. It begins with the assembly, not the preacher. The bishops call such a starting point not only appropriate but essential (#4). They offer two reasons. First, for communication to be effective, the partners in the communication must be known. Second and even more fundamental is the ecclesiological reason. Citing the *Dogmatic Constitution on the Church,* FIYH states that in the church "offices and ministries are necessary, but secondary. The primary reality is Christ in the assembly, the People of God" (#5).

FIYH proposed a radical strategy for engaging the assembly as subjects of the preaching: Involve members of the congregation directly in the preparation of the homily. This splendid idea is left underdeveloped in FIYH; that may explain why it has been so little heeded.

Preaching Basics

This book was, in large measure, inspired by the insight and innovation of FIYH — and inspired also by the way this document was never fully embraced either by bishops or by preachers.

Preaching Basics builds on FIYH. The goal is to improve the quality and consistency of liturgical preaching, especially in the Sunday assembly. First, we will ask the preacher and the community to consider together the unique nature of liturgical preaching, and their distinctive yet complementary roles in this event. Second, we hope to build confidence and enthusiasm by helping the preacher and assembly discover and integrate their particular gifts and insights into the preaching ministry. To this end, we will provide a clear, accessible, community-based model and method for homily preparation.

It is for you, the preacher, to do something with this. Even before you get too far into this introductory volume, share the materials and insights with key members of the pastoral staff, other preachers and members of your community so that together you might work more effectively for the transformation of the preaching event and of the liturgy which is its context and inspiration.

Authentic and effective liturgical preaching requires skills and preparation. It demands a commitment of time and an openness to criticism. Ultimately, however, it is not reliant upon the preacher's personality, proper technique or even theological skill. Rather it is a matter of passion, of heart, of love — both on the part of the preacher and on the part of the baptized assembly engaged in the preaching act. This is so because the God who is the source and summit of such preaching is One whose love for us is also a matter of passion and heart: epitomized in the passion of Christ and reborn in the heart of the resurrection. Let that paschal sermon, which we proclaim as the center of our faith, also be the source of our passion as we preach the reign of God, preach it into being.

Beginning with the Assembly

We believe that it is appropriate, indeed essential, to begin this treatment of the Sunday homily with the assembly rather than with the preacher or the homily, and this for two principal reasons. First of all we can point to the great emphasis which communication theorists place on an accurate understanding of the audience if communication is to be effective. Unless a preacher knows what a congregation needs, wants, or is able to hear, there is every possibility that the message offered in the homily will not meet the needs of the people who hear it. To say this is by no means to imply that preachers are only to preach what their congregations want to hear. Only when preachers know what their congregations want to hear will they be able to communicate what a congregation needs to hear. Homilists may indeed preach on what they understand to be the real issues, but if they are not in touch with what the people think are the real issues, they will very likely be misunderstood or not heard at all. What is communicated is not what is said, but it is what is heard, and what is heard is determined in large measure by what the hearer needs or wants to hear.

Contemporary ecclesiology provides a second and even more fundamental reason for beginning with the assembly rather than with the preacher or the homily. *The Dogmatic Constitution on the Church* describes the church as the mystery of God's saving will, given concrete historical expression in the people with whom God has entered into a covenant. This church is the visible sacrament of the saving unity to which God calls all people. "Established by Christ as a fellowship of life, charity, and truth, the church is also used by Him as an instrument for the redemption of all, and is sent forth into the whole world as the light of the world and the salt of the earth" (#9). The church, therefore, is first and foremost a gathering of those whom the Lord has called into a covenant of peace with himself. In this gathering, as in every other, offices and ministries are necessary, but secondary. The primary reality is Christ in the assembly, the People of God.

Fulfilled in Your Hearing, #4 – 5

Chapter Two

A Very Particular Genre

◼ Mapping the Terrain

Preaching is the proclamation of the reign of God. Any faith-filled act that announces the good news of salvation in Jesus Christ could be considered Christian preaching. Under this umbrella there are many distinct forms of preaching, of which liturgical preaching is only one.

An understanding of other types of preaching makes for a sharper notion of the special character of liturgical preaching. One helpful schema for developing this broader vision has been provided by John Burke and Thomas Doyle.[1] In addition to liturgical preaching, they suggest three other distinctive types of preaching: evangelization, catechesis and didascalia.

Evangelization   Burke and Doyle consider evangelization to be the basic form of all Christian preaching. Drawn from a Greek term that means "to announce well" or "to bring good news," evangelization is preaching addressed to

---

Catechesis

Can an athlete enjoy leisure once he has given in his name for an event? No, he trains and is anointed every day. He is given special food; discipline is imposed on him; he has to keep himself chaste. You too have given in your name for Christ's contest; you have entered for an event, and its prize is a crown. Practise, train, anoint yourself with the oil of gladness, an ointment that is never used up. Your food should be frugal, without intemperance or self-indulgence. Your drink should be more sparing for fear drunkenness should catch you unawares. Keep your body chaste so as to be fit to wear the crown. Otherwise your reputation may lose you the favour of the spectators, and your supporters may see your negligence and abandon you.

St. Ambrose, cited in Edward Yarnold, The Awe-Inspiring Rites of Initiation, *2nd ed. (Collegeville: Liturgical Press, 1994), page 15.*

Evangelization

Then Peter began to speak to them: "I truly understand that God shows no partiality, but in every nation anyone who fears him and does what is right is acceptable to him. You know the message he sent to the people of Israel, preaching peace by Jesus Christ — he is Lord of all. That message spread throughout Judea, beginning in Galilee after the baptism that John announced: how God anointed Jesus of Nazareth with the Holy Spirit and with power; how he went about doing good and healing all who were oppressed by the devil, for God was with him. We are witnesses to all that he did both in Judea and in Jerusalem. They put him to death by hanging him on a tree; but God raised him on the third day and allowed him to appear, not to all the people but to us who were chosen by God as witnesses, and who ate and drank with him after he rose from the dead."

Acts 10:34–41 (NRSV)

---

those who yet do not believe in Jesus, or those whose faith is nominal. The aim of evangelization is to move the non-believer or nominal believer to "an internalized faith-trust relationship to the Lord." We might imagine evangelization as a preaching style commonly employed by missionaries or televangelists. Given that such preaching is intended also for those who believe in name only, it is possible to imagine this type of preaching as an ordinary part of parochial life. For example, it might occur in the midst of religious education programs, as part of certain outreach events such as revivals, and even as an ordinary part of many weddings and funerals.

Catechesis   This is the next step in preaching, as it builds upon evangelization. Based on a Greek term for "oral instruction," Burke and Doyle distinguish catechesis from evangelization by its target group. Whereas evangelization addresses those whose faith in Jesus Christ is non-existent or nominal, catechesis presumes a hearer of the Word who has already begun to develop a relationship through the church with the One who is the source of that Word. Catechesis is directed toward the evangelized who have heard the call, and who seek "a deeper participation in the mystery of Christ among us."[2] In particular, catechetical preaching calls the newly evangelized to enter more deeply into the life of the faith community by embracing its teachings and participating fully in its sacramental life. At the same time, catechesis challenges the believer to integrate such teachings and liturgical practices with daily living. Gatherings of catechumens and even of the newly baptized would be appropriate settings for this type of preaching. It is possible, however, that such catechetical preaching might also be directed toward those who have recently experienced a renewal in their faith. Thus, those newly married or confirmed, as well as believers who have been reconciled with the church after significant absence, could benefit from catechetical preaching.

Didascalia   Burke and Doyle call their third category didascalia, which is a form of the Greek word for "teaching." Such preaching is directed toward those "already mature in faith whom God is calling to a fullness of relationship."[3] The aim here is to bring the believer into fullest union with God, or what traditionally has been called mystical union. It accomplishes this by providing the hearer with a more profound understanding of the Christian mystery, and by inviting complete participation in this mystery. The preaching that you might hear during a retreat or on a day of recollection would be one of the more common forms of didascalia.

Useful Distinctions   Often the preaching we hear at a parish mission or during some other kind of devotional service is a mixture of these genres. The point here is not to promote a rigorously differentiated use of these three genres of preaching. Rather, they are distinguished here as recognizable landmarks and helpful guides when mapping the preaching terrain. A clear understanding of these different categories of preaching helps us grasp more precisely the distinctive nature of liturgical preaching.

These three genres of preaching are primarily defined by their intended hearers. Neither evangelization nor catechesis nor didascalia requires any particular setting.

Liturgical Preaching

Liturgical preaching, while attentive to its intended hearers, is not essentially defined by the range or diversity of these hearers. Such preaching often occurs in the presence of precatechized or nominal believers. This is particularly true during occasional services such as weddings and funerals, and on great feasts like Christmas and Easter. Even the ordinary Sunday assembly is a mixed gathering of nominal believers, the recently evangelized and those with a more mature faith who are seeking deeper union with God.

Liturgical preaching is *defined by* and *bound to* the liturgy. This is the fundamental key to

---

Didascalia

Eucharist *means* thanksgiving. But the Eucharist is a genuine thanksgiving only if we ourselves become eucharists for the life of the world. Four verbs in each consecration spell out the rhythm in Christian discipleship. What Jesus did to ordinary bread at the Supper, that Jesus does to ordinary flesh and blood, to you. Jesus took, Jesus blessed, Jesus broke, Jesus gave. In giving you life, Jesus *chose* you to follow him. In your baptism Jesus *blessed* you, consecrated you to be his disciple. In your suffering Jesus *"breaks"* you, burns out the damnable concentration on self, remolds you to himself, shapes you as a man or woman for others. And so, wherever you are, Jesus *gives* you — chosen, blessed, and broken — gives you to a whole little world for its salvation. As the bread is transformed into Christ's body, do you feel your own flesh transformed into Christ, to share in his work of redemption?

Excerpted from Speak the Word with Boldness *by Walter J. Burghardt, sj. © 1994 by The New York of Province of the Society of Jesus. Used by permission of Paulist Press.*

such preaching. Those who undertake this ministry must understand and reckon with the pervasive manner in which their preaching is bound to and defined by its liturgical context. Even when such preaching needs to show some characteristics that we would associate with evangelization, catechesis or didascalia, these too must be caught up in the liturgical task and nature of this preaching.

Preaching is not "liturgical" because it occurs during the liturgy. That is, liturgical preaching is not preaching that occurs in the liturgy, but is preaching that is essentially of the liturgy. Liturgical preaching not only enables the unfolding of the liturgy and contributes to the overall purpose of worship, but is *itself* liturgy. At its very core, therefore, this preaching must be an act of worship.

Not Only "In" but "Of"

Unfortunately, much preaching during liturgy is not liturgical preaching. It occurs *in* the liturgy but is not *of* the liturgy. Those who would preach at liturgy need to attend critically to the relationship between the homiletic act and worship. One way to sharpen these skills and so develop a clearer understanding of the integral relationship between the homiletic act and the liturgical event is to underscore the disparity which commonly occurs between preaching and worship. Consider, for example, the following "non-forms" of liturgical preaching that sometimes trespass upon our worship:[4]

Liturgical preaching as public exegesis

The gospel today illustrates Matthew's reliance on Mark as its primary source, although Matthew provides us with characteristic differences and additions in his writings. This is because Matthew is writing for a different audience than Mark, and has a different theological agenda. For example . . .

Liturgical preaching as explanation of the current feast, season or ritual

As we celebrate this Chrism Mass we are reminded that there is evidence already in the fifth century that Thursday of Holy Week served as an important day for the consecration of oils within the Christian community. In

the third century Hippolytus of Rome provides evidence of the blessing of chrism, the oil of catechumens and the oil of the sick. It is true that in the Gregorian sacramentary . . .

Liturgical preaching as an opportunity to share one's personal story of faith

It was my grandmother who was the source of my vocation to the priesthood. She always prayed that I would be a priest, and made me promise her as she lay dying that I would one day be ordained. While my parents were against my going to the seminary, I knew that my sainted grandmother would guide me. My Mass of thanksgiving coincided with the anniversary of her death . . .

Liturgical preaching as an explanation of church doctrine

In the Nicene Creed which we recite each Sunday, we are given a special understanding of the relationship between the First and Second Persons of the Blessed Trinity in that classic formulation "God from God, light from light, true God from true God, one in being with the Father." This Athanasian formulation was in response to the heresy of Arius who, under the influence of the philosopher Plotinus, taught . . .

Liturgical preaching as an opportunity to rally the community

Today's gospel about the feeding of the five thousand could be considered a biblical invitation to the upcoming parish carnival. Now, what would that event have been like for Jesus if only fifty people had shown up? That's why we really need your presence Friday and Saturday. Like Jesus, we need the crowd, and, unlike Jesus, we need the money that the crowd will bring with them . . .

Liturgical preaching as moral exhortation

As it says in the gospel, "Woe to you, scribes and Pharisees." If Jesus were here today I am sure that in a similar way he would be saying to us, "Woe to you who say one thing and do another; woe to you who call yourselves children but do not help your elderly parents; woe to you who call yourself neighbor, but do not help your friend in need; woe to you who call yourself Catholic, but can never get to Mass on time . . .

Liturgical preaching as political lobbying

The reference in the responsorial psalm this day to the just who follows not the counsel of the wicked is an inspired affirmation of the candidacy of Tom Johnson, from this parish, who is running for election to the school board this November. Tom has been a member of our parish council and of own school board. He is a just man who contributes generously to this parish . . .

Liturgical preaching as local ecclesial news broadcast

As you may or may not have heard, Father Matthews from our neighboring parish, St. Lydia, has been sent away for rehabilitation. We should pray for him, as Saint Paul reminds us today in the second reading. We should also pray for the poor people of St. Lydia, who have suffered terribly under this strain, and for me since I am now required to say Mass over there every weekend . . .

Liturgical preaching as social activism

The touching story of Jonah and the whale, which was proclaimed as today's first reading, reminds us that whales, like all creatures of the deep, are our friends. Yet many of these magnificent creatures continue to die senseless deaths because of inhumane fishing practices. It is time to put an end to this systematic killing. A representative from Greenpeace will be in the vestibule after Mass . . .

The paradox is that while none of these is exactly on target, each makes a valid point. For example, while liturgical preaching is not essentially an exegetical exposition, it should be grounded in a credible interpretation of the day's scripture readings. Likewise, the liturgical homily is not a course in historical, doctrinal or moral theology, but it should be historically authentic, doctrinally sound and have clear ethical implications for the Christian life. Even the homily turned financial appeal or recruitment seminar underscores the need for such preaching to engage worshipers in building up the local community of faith.

The fundamental flaw in each of these approaches to liturgical preaching, however, is that they have not taken the liturgical event as their starting point. Instead they begin with exegesis, church doctrine, a moral perspective, the life of the parish, the transformation of society or some other element. While all of these find resonance in the liturgy, worship is not fundamentally an exegetical, doctrinal, moral, parochial or societal event. Rather it is a privileged moment for the divine-human encounter, and that encounter must be where all liturgical preaching commences. The Sunday liturgy is where this church, this assembly of the baptized, does what the Lord commanded. Over and over again, in the reading of the word, in intercession, in silence, in sung thanksgiving and praise, in holy communion, the mystery of our life in Christ is proclaimed and acclaimed. This is the encounter that is the ground of all liturgical preaching.

Let Him Tell Them the Truth

Let him tell them the truth. . . . Let him use words, but, in addition to using them to explain, expound, exhort, let him use them to evoke, to set us dreaming as well as thinking, to use words as at their most prophetic and truthful, as the prophets used them to stir in us memories and longings and intuitions that we starve for without knowing that we starve. Let him use words which do not only give answers to the questions that we ask or ought to ask but which help us to hear the questions that we do not have words for asking and to hear the silence that those questions rise out of and the silence that is the answer to those questions. Drawing on nothing fancier than the poetry of his own life, let him use words and images that help make the surface of our lives transparent to the truth that lies deep within them, which is the wordless truth of who we are and who God is and the gospel of our meeting.

Excerpt as submitted from Telling the Truth *by Frederick Buechner, pages 23–24. Copyright © 1977 by Frederick Buechner. Reprinted by permission of HarperCollins Publishers, Inc.*

A Definition from the Liturgy

If this is preaching *of* the liturgy, then it is to the liturgy itself that we must look for an appropriate definition for preaching.

The *Constitution on the Sacred Liturgy* (CSL) underscores central truths about the liturgy. Liturgy is:

- a celebration of the central mystery of the death and resurrection of Christ (#6)

- a way to give thanks to God for the inexpressible gift in Christ Jesus through the power of the Holy Spirit (#6)

- an action of Christ the priest and of the body of Christ, the church (#7)

- an experience of presence (#7)

- a fundamental source of the church's spiritual life (#12, 13)

Further, the liturgy presumes the full, conscious and active participation of all the baptized, which is both their right and their responsibility (#14). In a summary way, the CSL notes that the "liturgy is the source for achieving in the most effective way possible human sanctification and God's glorification" (#10).

The focus on Christ and the complementary language of presence and action in CSL suggest that the liturgy is meant to be the church's privileged and transformative encounter with God through Christ in the Spirit. Thus the assembly must be actively engaged in the liturgy, for they are not simply passive recipients of grace, but are graced through their dynamic engagement with God.

The whole of the liturgical event is to enable this. Preaching does not have a separate life or purpose. This complete integrity between preaching and its liturgical context means this: Preaching is an authentic act of worship.

While liturgical preaching cannot have a purpose separate from that of the liturgy which gives it life, it does have a distinct way of working. Preaching is verbal, but this is shared with reading and prayers. What distinguishes preaching from these other verbal forms is its conversational mode. As FIYH notes, the homily should sound like "a personal conversation, albeit a conversation on matters of utmost importance" (#68).

A Conversation between the Assembly and God

Liturgical preaching could be imagined as a kind of ritual conversation between the homilist and the assembly about God. But a better image would be this: Preaching as a ritual conversation between the assembly and God with the help of the homilist. Like the liturgy itself, this

---

Freed to Imagine

The sermon is not normally the place for concrete moral admonition, because such admonition will only enhance the partisan distortion, either in agreement or disagreement, rather than feed the imagination. Nor is the sermon the place for concrete instruction about public policy. Concreteness about policy questions, which is so crucial to the church, takes place more effectively in other contexts. The sermon is the place where the church is freed to imagine what it would be like to be intentional about mission and to embrace in our imagination acts of discipleship that we are not yet ready to accept in practice. Liturgy and proclamation precede, anticipate, and authorize our action in the world. Reflection about obedience in the sermon is more effective and compelling when it is bold and imaginative, well beyond our present capacity for action. Without such daring imagination, our action will stay in the pitiful and cowardly range where we live our timid lives. The spectacular cases of liturgy and proclamation leading to action in the world can be found in the contexts of Latin America, South Africa, and Poland, and in our own case in the Civil Rights protests. In those situations, liturgy and preaching have led to daring action for the sake of God's kingdom of justice and freedom. It is the imaginative anticipation of the gospel that invites us to many ways and places out of and beyond ourselves in missional caring for God's kingdom.

Reprinted by permission from Finally Comes the Poet *by Walter Brueggemann, copyright © 1989 Augsburg Fortress, pages 88–89.*

conversation is intended to be stimulating. The challenge for the preacher is to enable this dialogue between the church and God without attempting to act as surrogate for either. Part translator, part facilitator, part storyteller, the preacher keeps the conversation lively as those in this dialogue get to know each other more and more intimately.

FIYH says that liturgical preaching is like a conversation on matters of utmost importance. The subject of this conversation is the core of every liturgy: the death and resurrection of the Lord. Our Lord's death and resurrection are what we the church encounter when we place our whole selves, our whole lives, into the work of liturgy.

Thus the scriptures as presented through the lectionary readings and proclaimed in the midst of the church evoke innumerable facets of the faith. On a given Sunday the prophets or psalmist might stimulate a dialogue about justice or reconciliation. On another Sunday or festival, texts from Paul or Matthew might suggest a conversation that prods us to reconsider how we pray. The meeting of lectionary and life provides endless aspects, endless conversations and variations on the one subject, the essential mystery of faith: "Dying you destroyed our death. Rising you restored our life. Lord Jesus, come in glory." Ultimately the conversation needs to reckon with this abiding subject.

The lectionary readings are not alone in providing us with a multitude of wondrous images on their way to this single subject of the paschal mystery. Every facet of liturgy has this potential: the many prayers that we proclaim, hymns that we sing, gestures we enact, rites we perform, seasons we celebrate, feasts we keep, eucharistic prayers we proclaim. We often overlook the rest of this "liturgical bible."[5] This

is not to suggest that liturgical preaching is possible apart from serious dialogue with the readings. But more and more we recognize that the dialogue needs to be with the whole of the liturgy.

Liturgical preaching, this holy dialogue between God and church, must hold the attention of the church — this assembly. It requires special care with language. How do we speak of precious mystery and of extraordinary revelation in our ordinary speech? The dying and rising of Jesus Christ is the many-faceted jewel that must sparkle at the center of our liturgy and of preaching worthy of the liturgy. Without being self-conscious or artificial, the language that enables our ritual conversation must allow the beauty of that gem to filter through. Sometimes this breakthrough is achieved through simple narrative. Other times it may require a move to the poetic, or bold reliance on crisp language that wakes slumbering souls and puts drooping eyelids on gospel notice. Anyone engaged in "a conversation on matters of utmost importance" chooses words with care. Preachers can do no less.

Notes

1. John Burke and Thomas P. Doyle, *The Homilist's Guide to Scripture, Theology, and Canon Law* (New York: Pueblo, 1986).

2. Ibid., page 124.

3. Ibid., page 126.

4. This list builds on that given in Burke and Doyle, page 235.

5. This is a phrase borrowed from the writings of Louis-Marie Chauvet. See, for example, his *"La dimension biblique des textes liturgiques,"* in *La Maison-Dieu* 189 (1992): 131-47; we will explore this concept further in chapter three.

Preparing to Preach: The Model

■ What can we say of this particular genre of preaching called liturgical?

■ It can be imagined as a ritual conversation.

■ The topic of the conversation is nothing trivial.

■ This conversation takes place between God and a particular liturgical assembly.

■ It requires the mediation of a preacher.

■ Such preaching is itself a liturgical act.

■ It is shaped by the scripture readings and other elements of the "liturgical bible."

■ It requires an interpretation of those elements for the gathered community.

In a summary way, we could define liturgical preaching as a *ritual conversation between God and a liturgical assembly*. This conversation announces God's reign through the mediation of a preacher who offers a credible and imaginative interpretation of the liturgical bible in the context of a particular liturgy and community.

If we are comfortable with this definition, we can explore tools and techniques that systematically help the preacher work toward a fuller realization of such preaching. These are provided in the form of a model (in this chapter) and a method (in the next).

Why a Model and a Method?

Effective preaching is first of all a matter of passion: passion for the Word of God, passion for the liturgy and a particular passion for the baptized assembly. Acquiring and sustaining such passion, even when one is gifted (even when one is "inspired") in such things, is hard work. The preacher must recognize this! The gifts of the Holy Spirit do not negate our work, but rather sustain and encourage it. The model and method proposed here are a framework — a sustaining habit — as we build up our preaching ministry.

Think of what follows as proverbs and principles that require adaptation and nuance in each local community. Every good cook knows that a wonderful meal is not achieved by slavishly following every jot and tittle printed in the cookbook. Julia Child and the Frugal Gourmet often do not use measuring spoons or scales for ingredients, especially the spices. Instead they "measure" according to how it looks to the eye or feels in the hand. Their instructions are peppered with the words "approximately" and "about." So too with this preaching model and method. Adapt! Season to taste! Such is necessary if the preaching is to be a true feast for a particular community of faith.

The cooking analogy also provides a way to understand the distinction employed here between a model and a method. One might think of the model as the ingredients to be employed, and the method as the sequence for combining those ingredients.

Hilde's Chocolate Mousse
INGREDIENTS *(Model)*

    2 egg yolks
    1 12-oz package semisweet
        chocolate pieces
    1 cup scalded milk
    1/2 teaspoon finely ground decaf
        espresso beans
    3 oz. brandy
    4 egg whites
    1/2 cup sugar
    whipping cream

PROCEDURES *(Method)*

Put egg yolks, chocolate, milk, coffee and brandy in blender. Blend on high speed until the chocolate pieces liquefy. In a separate bowl beat egg whites, slowly adding sugar and beating till firm. Fold these into the chocolate mixture. Do not stir or beat. Refrigerate for at least two hours. Serve with whipped topping.

Hilde

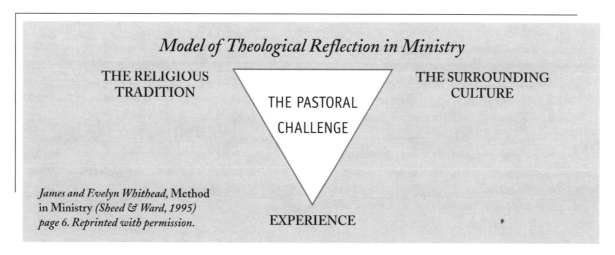

Model of Theological Reflection in Ministry

THE RELIGIOUS
TRADITION

THE PASTORAL
CHALLENGE

THE SURROUNDING
CULTURE

James and Evelyn Whitehead, Method
in Ministry *(Sheed & Ward, 1995)
page 6. Reprinted with permission.*

EXPERIENCE

This way of thinking about a "model and method" is borrowed from the classic by James and Evelyn Whitehead, *Method in Ministry.*[1] To provide an accessible guide to theological reflection, the Whiteheads distinguish between a model and a method. A model points to important sources of information for the work at hand. A method describes the dynamic or movement to be employed in doing the work.

In our approach to the ritual conversation called liturgical preaching, the model takes into account the partners in the conversation, while the method suggests how the conversation is to proceed.

The Model

Most preachers already have a model for homily preparation, although it may be more implicit than explicit. The challenge, therefore, may not be to create a completely new model as much as to make the current model explicit, examine it, critique it and expand it where necessary.

The model proposed here includes five major ingredients or conversation partners. These are the lectionary, the liturgical bible, world events, the arts and the human story.

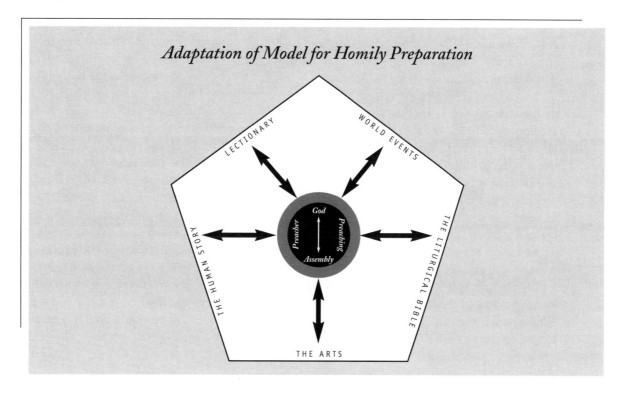

Adaptation of Model for Homily Preparation

LECTIONARY

WORLD EVENTS

THE HUMAN STORY

THE LITURGICAL BIBLE

God
Preacher — Preaching
Assembly

THE ARTS

The Lectionary

The lectionary readings are rightly the most respected element in liturgical preaching today. Based on principles articulated in the *Constitution on the Sacred Liturgy* (for example, CSL, 35), *Fulfilled in Your Hearing* (FIYH) considers the "word drawn from the Scriptures" one of the three major elements of liturgical preaching, the preacher and the gathered community being the other two (#3). This scriptural emphasis is woven into the document, and there is a section in FIYH dedicated to "interpreting the scriptures" (#25–30).

Cautions Most preachers today faithfully ponder the lectionary readings in preparation for preaching. Many consult commentaries or homily services in order to discern the meaning of these texts and successfully interpret them for their communities. Experience suggests several notes about the preacher's use of the lectionary.

First, much liturgical preaching today demonstrates a preoccupation with the gospel reading, sometimes to the exclusion of the other scriptural texts. This may happen because we give the gospel a prominence in the ritual and because it is the preacher who ordinarily proclaims the gospel in the assembly. Yet if the lectionary is a prime ingredient in liturgical preaching, then attention must be paid to all of the scripture texts: the three readings and the responsorial psalm.

Nothing is as helpful in this as a thorough understanding of the lectionary's structure. This is well explained in the Introduction to the lectionary (#58–69).[2] The basic plan of the Sunday lectionary should be so familiar that the preacher is always aware of it and able to speak from it.

Understanding the structure of the lectionary can greatly aid the preacher in seeing the continuity through each year's synoptic gospel, in discerning the linkage between the first reading and the gospel, and in respecting the second reading as a counterpoint to any given theme for a particular Sunday. The preacher's attention to all three scripture readings, as well as the psalm, is the foundation for a growing biblical literacy among all the baptized.

Awareness of the larger movement of the lectionary also sets one into a context where preaching can be organized over a number of Sundays as particular sections of the gospel or a New Testament letter are read.

The second reminder is this: Just as the liturgy in general cannot be reduced to any theme other than the death and resurrection of the Lord, so is it impossible to limit the lectionary readings to a single image or idea. Often it is the semi-continuous second reading which provides a useful counterpoint to the instinct to do so, and prevents any facile reduction of the day's readings to one idea.

Finally, the responsorial psalm should not be overlooked as an "integral part of the liturgy of the word."[3] The psalm, no less than any other scripture, is the word of God. As a source of prayer and reflection for the community in the midst of the readings, as well as an important interpretive key for discerning something of the linkage between the first reading and the gospel, it is a text not to be overlooked by liturgical preachers. Yet the preacher must also know that the lectionary does not dictate one specific psalm for each celebration, but allows some choice among alternative psalms.

Tools The lectionary texts are a rich resource for the preacher. They are also complex and they require the preacher's willingness to struggle with them. For this, the preacher should have basic skills and tools for understanding and interpreting the scripture texts. FIYH names some of these: an understanding — limited though it may be — of the original languages of these texts; a basic grasp of standard scriptural methods; a good biblical dictionary, a concordance, gospel parallels and standard commentaries on the major books of the Bible (#26 – 27).

While dictionaries, commentaries and even homily services can provide helpful exegetical information, they are no substitute for reading the lectionary texts themselves. The texts of the lectionary, not the texts about the lectionary, are the word of God. No matter how many times before the preacher has worked from and with them, these scriptures are always to be read freshly, carefully, repeatedly and out loud when preparing to preach.

The Liturgical Bible

Earlier we introduced the concept of the "liturgical bible."[4] This phrase is intended to include all of the liturgical elements that are not already included in the "lectionary" element.

We can begin with the words it includes. These are, for example, the eucharistic prayer, collects, the invariable (for example, the "Holy, Holy") and optional (for example, prayers for the blessing of an Advent wreath) texts of the liturgy, as well as the words of the hymns, songs and acclamations that are sung during worship.

But we go beyond this to think of the "liturgical bible" as more than the words. It also takes in ritual actions and objects and spaces, and even the feasts and seasons that we celebrate throughout the year. It is in this sense that we will be employing the term here.

CSL itself suggests that we give the liturgical bible such importance. In an often overlooked instruction, that pivotal document states: "Preaching should draw its content mainly from scriptural *and liturgical* sources." (#35.2, emphasis added)

Texts Longing to Be Preached

When we were lost
and could not find the way to you,
you loved us more than ever:
Jesus, your Son, innocent and without sin,
gave himself into our hands
and was nailed to a cross.
Yet before he stretched out his arms
between heaven and earth
in the everlasting sign of your covenant,
he desired to celebrate the Paschal feast
in the company of his disciples.

Eucharistic Prayer for Masses of Reconciliation I

In the midst of conflict and devision,
we know it is you who turn our minds to
   thoughts of peace.
Your Spirit changes our hearts:
enemies begin to speak to one another,
those who were estranged join hands
   in friendship,
and nations seek the way of peace together.
Your Spirit is at work
when understanding puts an end to strife,
when hatred is quenched by mercy,
and vengeance gives way to forgiveness.
For this we should never cease to thank and
   praise you.

Eucharistic Prayer for Masses of Reconciliation II

This assertion is echoed in the *General Instruction of the Roman Missal,* which notes that the homily should develop "some point of the readings or of another text from the Ordinary or from the Proper of the Mass of the day, and take into account the mystery being celebrated" (#41). The ground for this assertion is found earlier in the CSL when it announces that the whole of the liturgy — and not just the reading of the scriptures in the liturgy — is the fount and summit of the church's life.

In concrete terms, when have we heard a preacher take the text of the eucharistic prayer seriously? According to the *General Instruction of the Roman Missal* the eucharistic prayer is the "center and summit of the entire celebration" (#54). Ironically, this great center and summit seldom informs our liturgical preaching.

Examples This is not to suggest that the whole of the liturgical bible is always ignored in our preaching. Especially during occasional services or on high holy days we rely on this great treasury for our preaching. We instinctively know, for example, that at weddings the exchange of vows and the blessing and giving of rings are powerful symbols that can ignite an assembly's religious imagination and fuel the ritual conversation we call preaching. Similarly on a great feast like Christmas, we intuitively turn to lyrics from a favorite Christmas carol or traditional symbols like the crèche for homiletic inspiration. An appropriate method for preaching preparation should make an explicit and enduring place for what the CSL identifies as one of two central sources for our preaching.

The tradition has much to teach us about the importance of the liturgical bible for preaching. The homilies of the great fourth- and fifth-century preachers like Ambrose, Chrysostom and Leo are strewn with examples, citations and insights drawn from the liturgical bible. Augustine is one of the best examples of a pastoral theologian whose preaching is imbued with an abiding respect for the liturgical bible. Throughout his writings Augustine identifies over 300 "sacraments." He includes among these various catechumenal rites (for example, giving catechumens salt), feasts of the church such as Christmas, and devotional practices (for example, bending the knee). These "sacraments," drawn from the liturgical bible of his day, play an integral role in Augustine's preaching.

This is not to suggest that contemporary preachers should deliver a sermon on the importance of genuflecting or the meaning of the few drops of water that are put into the cup of wine at the preparation of the gifts. It does mean, however, that these gestures, actions, ritual texts and seasonal feasts need to be integrated into preaching. One of the reasons that much liturgical preaching seems unconnected with the rest of the ritual is that it does not acknowledge the rest of the ritual. The challenge is to integrate the two.

On the Twenty-ninth Sunday in Ordinary Time in Year B, when confronted with the text from Mark's gospel about the sons of Zebedee and Jesus' inquiry about whether or not they can drink from the cup that he is about to drink from, think about preaching on the significance of drinking from the cup at communion as a symbolic entry into Christ's death. During the Easter season, when the opening hymn is "Jesus Christ is risen today," might not such a text provide the preacher with a way to underscore the existential ("today," the great *hodie* of the church's liturgy) rather than the historical nature of the liturgical celebration?

We have defined liturgical preaching as a unique ritual conversation. An appropriate model for creating such a conversation needs to take the ritual — all of the ritual — seriously. Preachers, therefore, should not overlook the songs and texts, symbols and actions which constitute the liturgy. They are the very source of our faith (CSL, 10), and great conversation starters! When the preacher lives from the liturgy — from and within the whole array of Catholic rituals for marking time and space and life — then the preacher only needs to let this array enter the preaching conversation.

World Events

A third critical ingredient or conversation partner is the world and what is happening in it, from the local to the global. The Swiss theologian Karl Barth succinctly linked world events with preaching when, in one of the great preaching maxims of the century, he noted that effective preaching dictated having the Bible in one hand and the newspaper in the other. Liturgical preaching cannot ignore the world. Rather, it must acknowledge it and, when necessary, confront it.

FIYH strongly stresses the importance of this element for preachers:

> Preachers need to devote some time and energy to understanding the complex social, political and economic forces that are shaping the contemporary world. Watching the evening news on television or scanning the headlines of the daily paper may be a beginning but it is not enough. Preachers need exposure to more serious and sustained commentary on the contemporary world, the kind of exposure that can be gained through a program of reading

or through conversation with people who are professionally involved in such areas as business, politics or medicine. Without this kind of informed understanding of the complex world we live in, preaching too easily degenerates into platitudes of faith, meaningless broadsides against the wickedness of the modern world, or into an uncritical affirmation of the wonderful advances that have taken place in modern times. (#34)

This sustained conversation with our social, political, economic and entertainment environment is not simply a ploy for relevance or congregational appeal in our preaching. There is a strong theological reason for taking the world seriously in preaching. Karl Rahner was particularly eloquent on the vital bond between the liturgy and the world. He recognized that God's self-communication is not limited to the confines of certain ritual or devotional activities, but occurs throughout the whole of human history. Rahner taught that the world is permeated by the grace of God, and is constantly and ceaselessly possessed by God's self-communication from its innermost roots. This continuous self-communication of God through all of human history is what Rahner calls the "liturgy of the world."

> The world and its history are the terrible and sublime liturgy, breathing of death and sacrifice, which God celebrates and causes to be celebrated in and through human history in its freedom, this being something which [God] in turn sustains in grace by sovereign dispositions.[5]

Rahner's powerful notion of the "liturgy of the world" tells us that the linkage between liturgy and life is nothing casual. What we do in worship has serious implications for our actions. The liturgy and its preaching should make a difference in the way we vote, advocate for social change, challenge any decline in public morals and champion the cause of the powerless. Here we are formed for virtue, for good habits in making our world and ourselves the reign of God proclaimed in liturgy and preaching.

Taking the world seriously as a place of God's self-revelation is a two-edged sword. It affirms that the world is the arena in which we act out

Naming Grace

The absence of God is revealed to us when we realize that the world in which we are called to announce "good news" is not only limited but also wounded by sin and evil. In the face of that reality, naming grace becomes even more difficult. Here the preacher has no words of meaning that can make sense of what is senseless or that can defend what is indefensible as somehow part of "God's mysterious plan." The naming of grace can only follow upon silence and solidarity with those who suffer. The words of grace that well up from experiences of radical suffering are words of lament, grief, anger, and protest; they are anguished words of identification with the crucified one. If the voice of God is to be found here, it remains hidden in the human responses of protest and resistance. If the power of the Spirit can be detected, it is in the power of human endurance, compassion, and hope. The incarnation is the key to the sacramental imagination, but the history of the incarnation culminated in the tragedy of the cross. The art of naming grace has to do with proclaiming the cross in a world of radical suffering and evil.

In the end, however, it is not the cross that the baptized community proclaims but the paschal mystery of life that emerges beyond death. All that Christians have to live on are the stories and witness of those who have gone before them in faith and the power of the Spirit who keeps the story of Jesus alive. Naming grace means "naming the present" — trying to identify where the Spirit of God is active in contemporary human life and in communities of believers who make the gospel a concrete reality in limited and fragmentary, but still tangible, ways. In the end, preachers proclaim a word of promise, a word whose truth remains to be seen, a word of hope. In this sense preaching remains always a profound act of worship.

Excerpted from Naming Grace: Preaching and the Sacramental Imagination *Copyright © 1997 Mary Catherine Hilkert. Reprinted by permission of The Continuum Publishing Company.*

the implications of our worship and preaching, but taking the world seriously also allows the world, this revelation of God, to shape and even critique our worship and preaching.

How does a preacher engage this conversation partner? Whether introvert or extrovert, whether gregarious or contemplative by nature, the preacher cultivates discernment in a world where news has become entertainment. The preacher knows that the Christian's eyes are to be fixed just here and here and here — but knows also that we are often distracted. Attending to the scriptures and our tradition, we know what deserves our concern and what does not.

The preacher cultivates a probing attention in a world where news has become distraction. The preacher knows when some event in community or world is on everyone's mind, and the preacher knows when some event isn't on many minds but ought to be. The preacher has questions that go beyond the sound bites. Sometimes these questions are all we have to bring to the conversation, but they are terribly important. The prophets provide a model here: the justice of God toward oppressors and oppressed, the well-being of the poor, the health of the earth itself. These are some burdens the preacher bears in seeking a way to pay attention to the neighborhood and the whole universe. The preacher is not then full of self-righteous moral advice, but rather of questions and challenges known

firsthand. When the preacher must take a difficult stand, this will emerge from the larger process of preparing to preach (as described in the next chapter).

In such conversation with the world, the preacher is, through the years, able to discern what must be pointed out. The scriptures are never read in isolation, the liturgy never celebrated in a vacuum. What grows sharper with the years is the conversation that is made possible by a life attentive to the world's troubles and needs. More and more the conversation between scripture, liturgy and world can take place in the mind and heart of the preacher because of the habitual awareness that has been cultivated day in and day out, not for the sake of preaching alone, but for the sake of living a gracious life.

The Arts

Worship and the arts are intimately related. *Environment and Art in Catholic Worship* puts it well: "God does not need liturgy; people do, and people have only their own arts and styles of expression with which to celebrate." (#4) Over the centuries the liturgy has been a fount of artistic inspiration. It has moved builders to construct great cathedrals, composers to write enthralling music and craftspeople to shape beautiful vessels or design delicate glasswork. It has also inspired preachers over the centuries to ply their craft for the glory of God and the sanctification of the faithful.

Those who are privileged to shape the ritual conversation in worship today do so in the context of the arts: music, texts, architecture, glass, vesture and statuary. So it is difficult to imagine preaching without a sensitivity to the breadth of artistic disciplines that shape worship. How can one draw upon the liturgical bible, for example, without some appreciation for the music and movement that comprise that bible? Or how can one offer an appropriate interpretation of a lectionary text without some understanding of the literary genre in which the text is presented?

An appreciation of the arts is not some pleasant but wholly dispensable pastime for the preacher. It is a pastoral necessity in at least four different ways.

Knowing the vocabulary Without cultivation and appreciation of the arts, the preacher cannot engage adequately or respectfully with the liturgy that provides the essential context for this preaching. Thus FIYH notes: "Regular and sustained contact with the world's greatest literature or with its painting, sculpture and musical achievements can rightly be regarded by preachers not simply as a leisure-time activity but as part of their ongoing professional development." (#32)

The art of speaking Developing one's ability for artistic appreciation and understanding is also necessary if the preacher is going to fulfill the responsibility of providing a credible interpretation of the liturgical bible, which is central to our definition of preaching. Interpretation is an imaginative act. It requires making connections and providing fresh insights so that the conversation will continue. Preaching is not explanation. It is not repeating data. Preaching engages an assembly in conversation, and that is done only with the preacher's active imagination. Preachers have to exercise their imaginations outside of the preaching event if they hope to provide engaging interpretation of the liturgical bible within the preaching event. In view of this, maybe Barth's maxim quoted above needs to be expanded: Authentic liturgical preaching would seem to necessitate holding the Bible in one hand and the newspaper in the other, with music playing loudly in the background.

A storehouse FIYH provides a third reason why the arts are important for preachers: The arts provide a wealth of material which can be employed directly in the preaching act. "Dramatic presentations that deal sensitively with significant human issues can provide a wealth of material for our reflection and our preaching, both in its content and in its form." (#32) A great poet might give us powerful language for preaching. Thus William Butler Yeats's text about "a terrible beauty" could provide a new paradigm for preaching the passion on Good Friday. Or a film like "Babette's Feast" might provide a stunning analogy for preaching the true nature of eucharist on Corpus Christi.

Homilists hungry for fresh ideas need only immerse themselves in the arts. There they will find an often unexplored and virtually inexhaustible bounty.

Those who preach and those who help preachers prepare might develop accessible ways to hold onto the good texts that so often pass us by and can't be found when

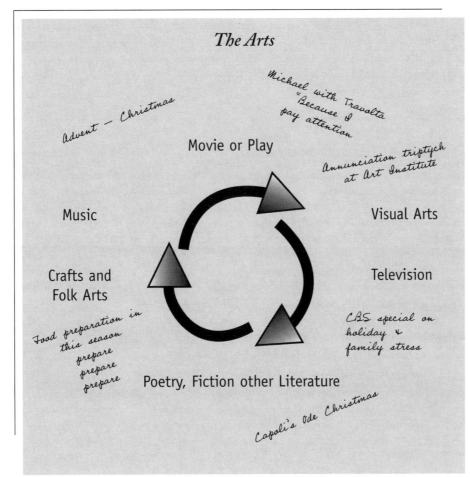

The Arts

Movie or Play

Visual Arts

Television

Poetry, Fiction other Literature

Music

Crafts and Folk Arts

Advent — Christmas

Michael with Travolta "Because I pay attention

Annunciation triptych at Art Institute

CBS special on holiday & family stress

Food preparation in this season prepare prepare prepare

Capoli's Ode Christmas

they are needed. Systems will vary, but whether on a computer or in a scrapbook, a preacher needs a way to keep and organize texts from a poem, a novel, an op-ed piece, a news story or any other source.

Art and the life of the assembly   Finally, as noted by FIYH, the arts are "a privileged means of access to the heart and mind of a people" (#31). It is well acknowledged that a society's art forms serve as cultural maps, revealing to the attentive observer the values and concerns of a people. Thus, while a careful scrutiny and analysis of the news and its commentary will provide the preacher with some understanding of the complex forces that are shaping the contemporary world, political reports and economic forecasts are not enough. The preacher also must enter the imagination of a culture, which is essentially achieved through a culture's arts.

This is not only true of the so-called fine arts, but also folk arts and popular forms of entertainment. All are indispensable for understanding the people to whom we are called to minister. As FIYH comments, this does not require spending long afternoons watching soap operas, memorizing sports statistics or listening to the latest hit songs. "Yet if we are totally unaware, or give the impression that we are unaware of the activities and interests to which people devote a good deal of their leisure time, energy and money, it will be difficult for us to make connections between their lives and the gospel, or to call them to fuller, richer and deeper levels of faith response." (#33)

Preachers are not expected to be connoisseurs or aesthetes. Season tickets to the opera or symphony do not a preacher make. On the other hand, preachers are required to develop their imaginations, grow in their understanding of culture and tradition and acquaint themselves with the people to whom they minister. It would be difficult to imagine accomplishing any of this without the arts.

The Human Story

If preaching is to be a ritual conversation between God and people, then both the divine and the human narratives need to be articulated.[6] In some respects these two story lines merge in the great tales of the Bible, are reflected in the wider liturgical bible and even interweave throughout the liturgy of the world in contemporary events and the arts.

These Books Speak of Every Human Situation

There are no two or three Bible passages that cannot be interrelated and that without verbal contortions to show the face of Christ, the *totus Christus* head and members. This is because the life, death and resurrection of Jesus are the life, sufferings and vindication of Israel writ large. But this life with its *misère* and its *gloire* is identical with the life of the church and all its members. Israel, come to completion through the aggregation of a gentile world to its small numbers, is "the mystery of Christ that was not made known to human beings in other generations but has now been revealed to his holy apostles and prophets by the Spirit" (Ephesians 3:5). This being so, it has to be possible to go from Scriptures, wisely used, to the lives of that segment of the church gathered for worship in this assembly on this Sunday morning.

Has there been a factory closing, the recent brutal murder of a child, an academic achievement by a local school, the death of a much loved member of the community, the joy of the season, the tragedy of nature gone amuck in flood or fire? To those who know the Bible well these books speak to every human situation. Homilists must know the Bible well. Only those who do so can draw on its riches at will, can employ convincingly the portions that appear in the liturgy of a feast or season.

Is there no place for the pertinent anecdote or the extrabiblical illustration that the homilist may find apt? There is, of course, but if it is trivial or frivolous it has no place in the homily. The thought that is profound as the Bible is profound — and it may come from a sphere termed "secular" — has every place there.

Gerard S. Sloyan, "Some Thoughts on Liturgical Preaching," Worship 71 (1997), pages 398-399.

Liturgical preaching is always in service of a particular community. So it is essential that the specific stories of that community and the individuals within that community receive explicit attention. It is not enough, therefore, for a preacher to have an overview of world events or major cultural events within a society. A preacher needs the flesh and blood narratives of the people who, Sunday after Sunday, gather to converse with God.

Human beings are storytellers. While there may be many reasons why stories have such potential for engaging us, a foundational explanation must be our narrative perception of human existence itself. We are our stories. They hold us together and keep us apart. Each of our lives is easily conceived as a web of stories. We think in narrative in order to weave together into a coherent whole the unending succession of people, dates and facts that fill our lives. The narrative mode fosters a sense of life and movement and process.

Storytelling is more than a useful genre for enhancing interpersonal communication: It is

Approach Them through Experience

If the story of Jesus Christ took place among the people, then the preaching of Jesus Christ must also find a place among the people; and since story involves the people whole — enticing personal commitment by the desire to hear the ending — it is story that can plant it there. It is not doctrines that comfort us in crisis. Nor are crises like examinations in school, attention to one isolated problem divorced from reality. It is Jesus himself who comes to comfort us, and crises are the dramas that swallow us whole, as the fish did Jonah. The stories of experience (themselves becoming experiences for the hearers) prepare the people to see God approach them *through* experience.

I don't want the doctrine of the resurrection. I don't even want the promise of the resurrection. Please: I want the *calmness* of the resurrection.

Excerpt as submitted from Ragman and Other Cries of Faith *by Walter J. Wangerin. Copyright © 1984 by Walter J. Wangerin, Jr. Reprinted by permission of HarperCollins Publishers, Inc.*

Nothing Like That Ever Happens in My Life

Once, at a preaching workshop, I noticed the look of frustration on a preacher's face when I spoke of the creative use of story in preaching. He finally raised his hand and complained: "Look, I work hard preparing my homilies. I know how important good preaching is. But where do I get the kind of stories, connections, illustrations that you are talking about? Nothing like that ever seems to happen in my life."

Robert P. Waznack, "The Preacher and the Poet," in Worship *60 (1986), page 47.*

also a key means through which we make sense out of life. We retell incidents, relate occurrences or spin tales not only to communicate what occurred, but more fundamentally to learn what truly occurred. Narrative is less about reporting than it is about discovering. We want to understand, we want to know some meaning, we want to find the sense in what has happened. Storytelling is a powerful instrument for interpreting the world and making it a habitable place.

Storytelling is a fundamental means by which human beings construct meaning, including religious meaning. We tell stories of God so that we might come to know God. And we tell tales of our encounter with God, so that we might learn how to encounter God. Worship — which is both a divine and human enterprise — makes an ample place for divine and human narratives. God's story needs to be told in scripture and prayer, story and song, steel and glass. Our story needs to be told as well, in all its particularity.

Preaching falls short at times because our gesture toward the human story is so generic that it does not resonate in a particular community. If, as FIYH notes, preachers need to know something about the activities and interests to which people devote a good deal of their leisure time and energy, how much more do we need to know something about the rest of their lives. It is not enough to know their baseball team; we need to know them.

What are their tales of joy and stories of grief? Whom have they loved and whom have they hated? What kind of work do they do? What do they think of their employment, and how does the job shape their family and their faith? Knowing the people may be the ultimate test and criterion for an effective liturgical preacher. Their lives are the particulars of Rahner's awesome liturgy of the world. Their struggles with family, employers, local government and the church are the terrible and sublime liturgy, breathing of death and sacrifice, which Rahner insists God celebrates and causes to be celebrated.

Happily for us, the Jesus of the gospels is an astounding model for any minister of the word. Over and over again Jesus enters into another's story, often simply sitting down to learn a name and share a meal. We often speak of Jesus as a storyteller, but first the incarnation of the Word was a consummate story-hearer. Those who wish to proclaim that same word today cannot help but be anything less.

An ear to hear the people of this assembly and of the larger community, *time* to hear — that also is part of the preacher's life. This is not done to build a repertoire of homily starters. It is done so that there can be preaching at all. The stories Jesus told were not retellings of the ones he heard at meals and along the road. But his stories were surely inspired by, sparked by, drawn out of all those stories he listened to. A preacher does not listen in order to retell but to know the depths of human life and so to speak from that as Jesus did. Little by little, the preacher discovers the best role of story in each homily, discovers how to tell those stories well. We have something to learn from the Garrison Keillors of the world, but that is how to tell a story, not necessarily how to preach.

The Conversation

These five conversation partners don't have an appointed time when they meet the preacher for coffee and talk. This amazing conversation is going on all the time in a preacher's mind and heart. It is a habit formed through years of practice, years of alertness, years of attention to the wonderful voices of lectionary, liturgy, world, art and community. Such conversation is an art, and the artist who practices it loves and dreads it at the same time. It can never be taken for granted. The art must be embraced in continuing practice. Practice, practice, practice!

Notes

1. James D. Whitehead and Evelyn Eaton Whitehead, *Method in Ministry: Theological Reflection and Christian Ministry,* rev. ed. (Kansas City: Sheed & Ward, 1995).

2. This important document can be found in *The Liturgy Documents,* published by Liturgy Training Publications.

3. *Introduction to the Lectionary,* #19.

4. See above, page 9.

5. Karl Rahner, *Theological Investigations XIV,* trans. David Bourke (New York: Seabury Press, 1976), page 169.

6. Much of what follows is reliant upon Herbert Anderson and Edward Foley, *Mighty Stories, Dangerous Rituals: Interweaving the Human and the Divine* (San Francisco: Jossey-Bass, Inc., 1997).

Chapter Four

The Preaching Event: The Method

■ From Commitment to Conversion

Preaching requires commitment, even passion: for the Word of God, for the liturgy, for the assembly. For most of us, this passion needs a structure to sustain it. Such a structure or method is the subject of this chapter.

Before going into the details of that structure, two things must be accomplished. First, a reflection on the true (and wonderful but scary) conversion that many preachers need as they embrace this approach to preparation. Second, "Attending, Asserting and Pastoral Decision-Making" gives an overview of what is going on as we then talk about Remote Preparation, Intermediate Preparation and Immediate Preparation.

This book includes an appendix of homiletic exercises. These are intended to help with various aspects of preaching preparation. In each parish situation, some will work as they are, some will need adapting, some will not be needed. These can be reproduced by the parish purchasing this book.

Conversion to method Model is distinguished from method here just as ingredients in a recipe are distinguished from the order of combining and mixing used to produce the final product. Most liturgical preachers have at least an instinctive number of elements or ingredients they ordinarily use. These may include a story or illustration, some exegesis, reference to some pressing social issue. In the previous chapter we noted five major ingredients or conversation partners in effective liturgical preaching: the lectionary, the liturgical bible, world events, the arts, the human story. The challenge to liturgical preachers is to make their own model explicit, to examine and critique it in view of these five essential elements and correct or

expand it where necessary. (See exercise 1 below and in the back of this book.)

Many preachers seem to have in place a regular and considered process or sequence for combining these ingredients. Liturgical preaching is significantly enhanced when model is joined to method, and the "ingredients" are combined according to some reflective sequence. FIYH recognizes this:

> The total amount of time we spend preparing may be less important than our observance of a regular pattern of activity spread out over a certain period of time. A regular daily pattern of activity for the preparation of the Sunday homily is . . . often the key

---

exercise 1: The Conversion to Method

You have a method for preparing to preach. Outline it here, including the variables things you sometimes do. Try to make explicit what may be only implicit. You may wish to think of this as handing on your own recipe.

First list the ingredients. Think of these as your own conversation partners (which may differ greatly from those discussed in Chapter 3).

1. *scripture*
2. *commentaries*
3. *a good story*
4. *homily helps*
5.

etc.

Then write your recipe, noting the approximate time given to each step.

	time
1. *read scripture*	*10 min*
2. *look at homily helps*	*20 min*
3. *read commentaries*	*15 min*
4. *write the sermon*	*30 min*
5.	

What works in this recipe?	What does not work in this recipe?
1. *attention to scripture*	1. *too heavy on scripture*
2.	2. *I do it all alone*
3.	3.
4.	4.
5.	5.

---

factor in effective preaching over the long term. (#82)

Thus the first conversion for the preacher is to a method in preparation.

Conversion to time   A second conversion concerns the time the preacher spends in preparation. This preparation is often something which occurs sporadically for the busy pastoral minister. As the weekend looms closer, pressure grows to carve out a few thoughts. For many preachers on many Sundays, the results are disappointing. What goes wrong when the preacher works at the last minute?

As an imaginative and interpretive act, preaching is more like a work of art than a commodity which can be efficiently produced under pressure. It requires some ordering of time for development and refinement.

But this conversion to time is not primarily about the total time it takes to be ready to preach. It is about the gestation period necessary for generating preaching that is consistently good. Most preachers rush to finalize their thoughts and finish the sermon rather than allowing time for these thoughts to develop. The assembly then hears what should have been a rough beginning as a final product. Enabling a ritual conversation between an assembly and God means that preachers allow sufficient time to produce a worthy sermon, a hard-won twelve minutes when God and assembly can truly converse.

In the method proposed here, the spacing between the various moments or stages is more important that the total time spent in preparing to preach. Just as grapes need time to ferment and dough needs time to rise, so does preaching require its own period of development. Below we will suggest three major stages in the evolution of a liturgical sermon: remote, intermediate, and immediate preparation. Spacing between those stages is critical. You can't skip the stewing stages.

Conversion to collaboration   This entire examination of liturgical preaching has been cast in terms of a dialogue, not a monologue. It has emphasized embracing the assembly as a subject rather than an object of preaching. Liturgical preaching — like the very liturgy which serves as the defining context for such preaching — is not a product the preacher provides *for* the assembly, but a dialogue which the preacher forges *with* the assembly.

Can the preaching event be this dialogue if the preparation for that event is not also a dialogue? Often the preparatory dialogue for the preaching event is informal or unplanned. We hear a story about some episode in a parishioner's own life which seems to echo the scriptures and the season in some way. A memorable encounter in reconciliation or marriage preparation provides a counterpoint or illumination of the day's lectionary and liturgical texts. Such chance meetings are often a boon to our preaching. When they occur we make a mental note, or jot down the insight for inclusion in the liturgical sermon.

But happy coincidence won't get us through the long haul. Because worship and preaching have dialogue at the core, the assembly's role in the preparation of the preaching must be more than a happy coincidence. Input from the liturgical assembly should be neither a matter of chance nor icing on the cake. Rather, their word and their world needs to be integrated into the preparation process. The assembly's voice must find a place in the preaching method.

FIYH notes that "an effective way for preachers to be sure that they are addressing some of the real concerns of the congregation in the homily is to involve members of that congregation in a homily preparation group" (#106). Such a homily preparation group is the engine that drives the method described below. Before turning to such particulars, however, the liturgical preacher must embrace collaboration as a nonnegotiable in the preparatory process. (See exercise 2 in the back of this book.)

Attending, Asserting and Pastoral Decision-Making

The method developed by James and Evelyn Whitehead for theological reflection provides a framework for thinking about preparation to preach. Their method has three components: attending, asserting and pastoral decision-making.[1]

Attending   Sometimes preachers, like other pastoral ministers, move to a decision without the benefit of careful listening. The attending stage is a time of listening critically to the various conversation partners. This is listening with care and respect. And it is listening while suspending judgment. It is crucial to understand from the outset that attending and decision-making are two very different stages in this method.

The liturgical preacher attends conscientiously to the five conversation partners: the lectionary, the liturgical bible, world events, the arts and the human story. In our method, attending receives special attention during remote preparation.

Asserting   Asserting means gathering the various perspectives acquired during the attending process into a dialogue of mutual clarification and critique. Recalling our recipe analogy, the assertion moment could be considered a time of fermentation or stewing. Here the elements age and simmer together. It is a time when ideas interact and mature. In preaching preparation, this translates into enough time for images from the liturgical season, texts from the scriptures, people's stories of faith and crisis and the other conversation partners in our proposed model to all stew together, to ferment. Let them interpret one another imaginatively. Let them critique one another. In our method, the asserting stage will receive special attention during intermediate preparation.

The Whiteheads note that the conversation at the assertion stage presupposes some mutuality among the conversation partners. Failure is likely when one attends only to one source of information.[2] Appropriate asserting demands that we respect all of the conversation partners in this preparatory process, and allow each element to season the others as the liturgical sermon matures.

Pastoral response   In the Whiteheads' method, this is "moving from discussion and insight to decision and action." Such is accomplished by focusing on the best insights of the assertion stage. Only now at the end of the process comes the making of decisions. In our method, pastoral response receives particular emphasis during the time of immediate preparation.

Remote Preparation: From Attending to Asserting

We come now to the three stages of our method. These are chronological and correspond roughly to the three tasks of attending, asserting and making a pastoral response. Given the nature of the lectionary and of the liturgy itself, these stages are not conceived as rigidly applying to every Sunday. Rather, the remote (attending) and intermediate (asserting) stages of preparation will be of particular importance when thinking about a whole liturgical season or group of Sundays through Ordinary Time. The pastoral decision-making stage, on the other hand, especially comes to bear at the end of the asserting stage and during the time of immediate preparation.

Goal   The goal of remote preparation is to generate sufficient ideas and insights about preaching during the coming liturgical season so that, at the next stage in the process, a specific plan for this preaching can be decided upon.

When?   The attending phase is for listening critically to the various conversation partners. The preacher is a listener and this means conscientiously listening to the lectionary, the liturgical bible, world events, the arts and the human story. If there is to be adequate time for the later phases of the preparation, this initial act of attending must take place long before the preaching.

The liturgical year itself helps set these times. This is so because individual Sundays aren't entities unto themselves. They are part of a flow in the lectionary and the liturgical bible. This is especially so during the seasons of Advent and Christmas, Lent and Easter. But it is true also in Ordinary Time. The shape of the church year dictates to a large degree the structure of the Roman lectionary. Thus, preparation for liturgical preaching is not simply preparation for a single Sunday or feast of the year, but preparation of a plan for preaching throughout an entire season. As FIYH notes, liturgical preaching is often ineffective because each Sunday's homily is preached "as if it had no connection with what preceded or what will follow" (#85). If we pay close attention to the shape of the liturgical year, we will diminish this tendency toward discontinuity.

Begin the remote preparation well in advance of the season under consideration (and by "season" is meant any series of Sundays even in Ordinary Time). Advent preparation, for example, needs to begin around the middle of October. This attending phase begins with a single gathering, followed by a few weeks of reflection and simmering.

Who? The collaborative nature of preaching and its preparation suggests that this attending cannot be achieved by the preacher alone. It is important to gather others to help forge as broad an overview as possible of the lectionary texts, various elements of the liturgical bible, community events and other components. There are a number of ways to constitute such a group, but it should always include all of those who will be preaching during the season.

Besides the preachers, invite a few thoughtful, articulate parishioners. Cultivate imaginative people for the group; some may be well educated, others may not. In the process, look over the conversation partners (the lectionary, the liturgical bible, world events, the arts, the human story). Ask, for example, if there is a person in the parish who regularly follows current affairs and who might bring insight in the area of world events. In the area of the human story, ask if there is a person who is the chronicle-keeper of the parish, the one who knows much of what happens in people's lives. Would such a person be a good participant in these meetings?

The mix itself can be a great factor in success. It may be important to include one or more members of the parish council, key members of the parish staff (for instance, the liturgy or music coordinator, the director of religious education, the coordinator of social programs), the lector coordinator. But don't let the group get too large. Different persons can be invited for the next season. It might be helpful to rotate people on and off as FIYH suggests (#106), so that fresh ideas and new perspectives continue to enliven and renew the preaching within a community. But continuity is important also, as many become better at this work with practice.

Sometimes there is a temptation to gather only clergy from the surrounding area or only professional ministers. While this is certainly helpful — and a *much* better procedure than preparing for preaching alone — every effort should be made to engage a true representation of the local community. This does not need to be a large group. A group of five or six is ideal: Fewer than four may provide too narrow a spectrum of viewpoints, while a group of ten or more becomes unwieldy.

How? The success of the remote preparation is, to a large extent, contingent upon the willingness and ability of the group members to contribute imaginatively and reflectively to the process. This means that they must come to the gathering prepared. They will have reviewed the elements outlined in the model; that is, they have read the

Sunday	Reading I	Psalm	Reading II	Gospel	Posture/Gesture	Sacramentary
Advent 1	climb the mountain	go	wake	coming prepared	can't sit	opening prayer: Searching for Light
II	Sprout signal for maker		patience	Prepare Baptize		Preface I watch for the day
III	Exalt Bloom Love Leap		Patient don't grumble	Prophet report what you see & hear	Preface I watch for the day	Preface I watch for the day

scriptures and other liturgical texts of the season, and have thought about the prevailing issues of the local community. (See exercises 3 and 4 in the back of this book. A partially completed sample similar to exercise 4 appears as a sidebar at the bottom of pages 24–25.)

The group needs to be reminded early on that the purpose of the gathering is more exploration than decision-making (the pastoral response), more attending than asserting. Remote preparation is a time of brainstorming and stimulating the imagination rather than deciding. It is a time to ask larger questions about the style and tone of the preaching through the season. For example:

■ What difference does it make at this time in the community's history that we are hearing readings from a particular lectionary cycle, gospel writer or prophet?

■ What topics for their ritual conversation does this community need to consider in the coming season?

■ Are there particular rituals in this season which could or should have an influence on the preached word?

■ Have there been important local or national events, crises or images that need to be woven into the preaching?

■ Are there elements of the environment and the music that have become traditions for these seasons and so can contribute to or enliven the preaching?

The Whiteheads suggest that there is a value to beginning theological reflection by first attending to human experience. In preparation for Advent preaching, for example, it may be good to begin by praying for the community which is to be engaged in this ritual conversation. After invoking God's Spirit upon that community and those who minister to it in preaching, assess the current mood and spirit of the local community. Is this a time of special economic hardship, high energy or unusual discord in the community? Are we experiencing major changes? Does the parish experience an influx of visitors or returning family members during this season? What difference does the composition and disposition of the assembly during this season have on the shaping of the preached word for this season? How does the stance of the community serve as a lens through which the readings are perceived, or a context in which the official liturgy is engaged? (See exercise 5 in the back of this book.)

After this initial exploration around what we have called the human story, it might then be helpful to turn to the lectionary and the liturgical bible together. It is often wise to read aloud a number of the season's scriptures, even though people have been asked to read all the Sunday scriptures beforehand. This establishes the foundational work of the lectionary. People are asked to listen for what strikes them. Time is needed to let people speak of strong images from these texts. Then read aloud a few key texts from the

Special Rituals	Melodies & Sung Texts	Environment	Special People/Groups	Other	
Blessing about wreath	Come— O Come Emmanuel		catechism	children's liturgies	Look at verbs
		special lights?			
	ask Mary	hospitality colors?	Lots of visitors		

liturgical bible: an opening prayer or two, a preface and maybe a proper blessing or a key seasonal song text (or sing this). What are the prophetic images employed in the sacramentary's prayers for the season that could shape a ritual dialogue for this community at this moment in their history? Is it a word of repentance, or an announcement of hope or a call to mission that they could and should hear? How might, for example, the lighting of the Advent wreath, or texts from some of the great Advent hymns or the use of Eucharistic Prayer I for Reconciliation provide a resource or thread to the seasonal preaching? (See exercise 6 in the back of this book.)

Next turn to a consideration of larger social and political events in the world. Is the region or the country confronting particular challenges or celebrating fresh achievements? Are there impending elections, and what will that mean for the community? Has there been a rash of hate crimes or renewed racial prejudice that needs to be addressed? And where are there signs of hope in the world: peaceful elections, acts of reconciliation, blessings or awesome acts of courage and compassion? How do these spark a message of Advent, a word of preparation, a ritual dialogue that engages a community at the heart of the season? (See exercise 7 in the back of this book.)

Finally, what elements of a community's artistic and cultural life might inform the preaching? Is this the time when beloved classics like Handel's "Messiah," Tchaikovsky's "The Nutcracker" or Dickens' "A Christmas Carol" are performed in the city or region? Are there recent films, short stories, television specials or fresh poetry that can charge the preaching? Does your community stage pageants, engage in particular folk arts for this season or produce special crafts or food during Advent? And how might these give texture and flavor to the preaching which itself is crafted to the season? (See, for example, the sidebar on page 17. Use this model or one like it for seasonal homily preparation.)

It is quite possible, with good leadership, to move through such a process in about 90 minutes, especially if people come prepared. Lively and to-the-point discussion is always more effective. Leadership has to keep the discussion from wandering too far, from getting ponderous, from being taken over by two or three people.

A designated member of the group should be responsible for taking notes during this brainstorming process. These notes will be important in the next two stages of preparation.

Intermediate Preparation: From Asserting to Pastoral Response

Goal   The goal of intermediate preparation is to reach consensus on a plan for preaching during the approaching season.

When?   Remote preparation, culminating in the single meeting described above, has stirred the pot, stimulated ideas and begun the imaginative and reflective processes necessary for asserting and then pastoral decision-making. Intermediate preparation (the assertion stage) begins with the end of the initial preparatory meeting. Following that meeting, the members of the preparation group individually continue a process of prayer, reflection and assertion.

This means gathering the various insights and resources which surfaced at the initial preparatory meeting into a dialogue of mutual clarification and critique so that a clear direction for preaching through the coming season can be developed and shaped.

Two to three weeks following the initial meeting, the planning group convenes a second time.[3] Since the goal of this meeting is to provide an overview of the preaching for the approaching season, the group asks:

- What are the images that are going to be highlighted from week to week?

- What are the motifs that need to be woven from Sunday to Sunday?

- What connections should be made between the various Sundays and their preaching during the season?

- What is the appropriate progression for the preaching through this period?

This second meeting marks the transition from the asserting process to pastoral response. Sufficient time between the first meeting and this one allows the members of the group to weigh the various options and consider the pros and cons of one direction or another. Placing the meetings less than two weeks apart could mean that the second meeting only continues the first. That is not what is intended. However, putting too much time between the first and second meetings could allow the process to become unfocused.

Who?   Because the purpose of this meeting is to forge a direction for preaching based on an attending and asserting process initiated at the previous meeting, it seems inappropriate to add new members to the group at this time. Given the reality of pastoral ministry today, it is likely that some of the members from the first gathering will be absent for the second gathering. Structure the first group just a little larger than the ideal number to ensure a strong gathering for the second meeting. The meeting should not be held at a time when any one of the homilists would have to miss it.

How?   In order to arrive at a consensus around a basic preaching design for the season, the group can do four things.

First, prayerfully call to mind again the community for whom this work is being done, and ask for God's wisdom in this preparation process and the preaching that is to follow.

Second, review the ideas generated at the previous brainstorming session as a part of remote preparation. This is an effective way to stimulate people's memory and launch the group anew into this process.

Third, each participant should be given some time to report how their thoughts about preaching through the upcoming season have developed or changed since the last meeting. In particular, individuals should be encouraged to discover if there were any convergences or confirmations of ideas from the first meeting through the intervening weeks. In preparing preaching for the Advent season, for example, did members of the preparation group get a sense that the present economic or social reality of the community suggests emphasizing the eschatological and hopeful aspect of the coming season? Or, does this community need to be prophetically challenged to reconciliation, which also is a strong motif of the season?

Fourth, the group engages in an explicit process of assertion. Brainstorming ideas have been recalled, developments in thinking have been shared. Now it is time for a critical conversation about the pros and cons of one preaching plan or another. The group needs now to come to some consensus about the direction of the preaching for the coming season. The goal here is to discover some convergence of ideas and energy around a preaching strategy. Often it becomes clear that there may be more than one possible direction for a community. The group must choose a single direction. Ideas that are not accepted for this year need to be noted and stirred into the conversation next year where they might provide impetus for preaching. (See exercise 8 in the back of this book.)

In coming to a decision about the preaching strategy for a season, the group should settle on some direction for the season, note how that direction will progress from Sunday to Sunday, and where possible provide the individual preacher resources for fleshing out this direction when it comes time to shape individual homilies. For example, during the coming Advent season, a group may have decided that given the rash of hate crimes in the city and the strong images in the readings of Year C around justice and repentance, the season's preaching should emphasis the intimate connection between the reign of God and justice. In particular, on the First Sunday of Advent attention to the reading from Jeremiah and the psalm could allow the community to consider human justice as a reflection of God's justice, particularly revealed in Jesus. Turning to the second Sunday, we are reminded that the true joy of the season comes from mercy and justice, not from consumerism and the acquisition of goods, which is a very strong message from the marketplace before Christmas. On the third Sunday, the witness of John becomes the Christian model for straight talk about treating our neighbors justly. And on the fourth Sunday, the true justice of God, revealed in Jesus, is not one of simple externals but conversion of heart.

Evaluation Evaluation is an essential part of this preaching ministry. Like the scrutinies we celebrate during Lent, evaluation should bless what is good and acknowledge where there has been failure and need for conversion. Evaluation sometimes works as part of the assertion stage, and so is recommended here. While a new preaching plan is being forged for the coming season, the previous plan is briefly reviewed as a way to recall what is effective in preaching for this community, and what is not. (See exercise 9 in the back of this book.)

It is also possible that the evaluation process might be part of the attending stage. For example, recalling the previous preaching plan (as well as the various ideas generated around that plan that may not have been used) is another way of stirring the imagination of the group, commending what was good and recommending change where experience suggests a better course.

In some places it will be more beneficial to reconvene the group after the season under consideration has ended for an evaluation session.

Whenever it occurs, the evaluation should be a brief yet pointed assessment of the previous preaching strategy and its implementation. Questions that could aid this evaluation are:

- How effective was the plan for the previous season?

- Was the focus or direction accessible and helpful to the community in their ritual conversations at worship?

- How well was the plan communicated and addressed by individual preachers?

- What could be learned, repeated or changed in view of the strengths or weakness of the previous plan?

Immediate Preparation

Goal The goal of immediate preparation is the actual crafting and preparation of the preaching for a specific Sunday or feast.

When? The immediate preparation takes place the week before the preaching. We presume here that this immediate preparation flows out of the two seasonal meetings described above.

Immediate preparation for preaching on the First Sunday of Advent, for example, begins on the preceding Monday and continues through the whole of the week. Previously we noted FIYH's emphasis that the total amount of preparation time is less important than the pattern of preparation spread out over a determined period of time. When considering the period of immediate preparation it is especially helpful to recall FIYH's insistence that a regular daily pattern of activity in preparation for preaching on Sunday is often the key factor in effective preaching (#82). This means that in the week prior to the preaching event, the preacher needs to devote time each day to the preparation of the liturgical sermon. The amount of time may only be fifteen minutes on some days, but it should occur regularly through the week.

Who? The immediate preparation is essentially accomplished by the individual preacher. The preacher has participated in the remote and intermediate meetings and processes, and it is now time for the preacher to craft, practice and enact the preaching event. This does not mean, however, that collaboration is suspended during this period. The preacher must continue to be in dialogue with the thoughts and ideas, suggestions and brainstorming, mapping and strategizing that the preparation group generated. Furthermore, the preacher should continue ad hoc consultation, especially with those who shared in the remote and intermediate processes, through this last phase of preparation.

How?   The experience of the remote and intermediate processes of preparation should provide the preacher with a variety of ideas and insights and even imperatives that can shape the preaching. In particular, the preparation group's agreement on a particular preaching strategy for a season and a general overview of the progression of this strategy from Sunday to Sunday provide the broad parameters for shaping each preacher's words during this season. Suggested steps for moving from this general overview and progression to a single sermon follow.[4] (See exercise 10 in the back of this book.)

Monday's review   First the preacher needs to review the materials that generated the seasonal plan and progression in the first place. The preacher should give special attention to the texts both from the lectionary and the liturgical bible. As FIYH proposes, prayerfully read and reread the lectionary readings, and do so out loud (#86). Also read the relevant texts from the liturgical bible for the day. Of particular import are the opening prayer and the eucharistic prayer (including the preface). Include the lyrics of songs and chants being used the next Sunday. Consider also the texts of any special rites being celebrated that day. In Lent this could include the rite of election or the scrutinies, in Easter the thanksgiving over the water at the sprinkling rite. Then pause to think beyond the texts. Think about the music, gestures, objects, environment and all other non-verbal elements of the ritual.

As in previous moments of preparation, look for convergence in the texts. Where do the images refract, counterpoint or support each other? In particular, where is there convergence between these primary texts and the direction outlined for the season by the planning group? As FIYH suggests, jot down ideas and connections as you read the texts. These jottings will become important in the week's further work.

Tuesday's study   After reviewing the plan and reading the key liturgical texts, it is valuable to turn to commentaries, explanations and expositions of these texts. This certainly includes biblical commentaries, but it does not end there. The lectionary is a particular use and juxtaposition of biblical texts; the preacher will find it helpful to read commentaries on the lectionary as well as standard biblical commentaries. Furthermore, there are fine resources that discuss the readings within the context of the larger liturgical bible.[5] Consulting commentaries across the spectrum of the biblical and liturgical texts will contribute much to generating a healthy conversation between these different dialogue partners.

Take notes through this process. Keep alert for any dovetailing between commentaries under consideration, your own thoughts from Monday's review and the preaching plan for the season.

Wednesday's outline   By the middle of the week, sketch the broad lines of the sermon. Images and stories, exegetical insights and inspiration from the season need to be shaped into some progression. Since preaching is a ritual conversation between the assembly and God, it might be useful to look for a good discussion starter to begin the preaching. Is there a recently heard story, an arresting artistic image, a powerful news item that can engage the community at the very start? As you shape the outline, you may discover gaps or places where connections need to be refined. You may find, for example, that you do not have any illustration that will enflesh that necessary conversation partner, the human story. Attempting a rough outline in mid-week gives you time to look for that illustration, informally consult with members of the preparation team and test out an idea or two before setting it in stone.

Thursday's stewing   Preaching preparation takes time and takes space between the times. A stewing period has been part of the process all along. In the final stages of immediate preparation, before drafting the text, it can be helpful to step back from the work and, in the words of FIYH, "give free rein to the subconscious processes" (#92).

If you are inspired, you may want simply to move into drafting the text you will preach Sunday. On the other hand, your outline might suggest that you need to consider further connections between texts and season, world events and the ethos of the local community. Are there gaps in your outline that need to be filled in? Does the progression make sense? Give yourself some time to step back and consider.

Friday's drafting Gathering your notes and ideas, materials from the preparation meetings and your reconsidered outline, do a full draft. For some this might mean writing out the text in complete sentences. For others it could be a complete outline. Use the form that is most comfortable for you. The task here is to get the progression, key metaphors and illustrations down on paper. Since there is time the following day to refine the text, it is not essential that every phrase be perfect, or every transition smooth. Developing your complete text or outline at this point, however, is essential.

Saturday's practice and refinement Preaching is auditory. While the outlining or writing is essential, you must practice the text out loud in order to make the transition from text to event. This will help you refine and critique the text.

Read the text over a few times, and then step away from it and try to speak it without reading it. Where is it easy to remember? What transitions or language seem awkward? Where does the sounding out of the text call for refinements or changes in the written script? The move from writing to speaking in the preparation process is an essential rehearsal for the preaching itself. Whether or not you have the final script in front of you for the actual preaching event, a liturgical sermon is not to be read. It is to be spoken, proclaimed and narrated. Liturgical preaching as outlined here is essentially a conversation. The preacher, therefore, needs both to prepare and rehearse in the manner of a public conversation: out loud, and with the focus on the participants and not on the page.

Notes

1. What follows is reliant upon pages 13 – 16 in the Whiteheads' *Method in Ministry*.

2. Whiteheads, page 83.

3. If the original gathering of the group was five to six weeks before the beginning of the liturgical season under consideration, this second and final meeting of the group occurs two to three weeks before the start of that season.

4. Some of what follows is inspired by the seven-step method for homily preparation outlined in FIYH: 1) reading, listening, praying, 2) study and further reflection, 3) letting go, 4) drafting, 5) revising, 6) practicing and 7) preaching (#86 – 105).

Preparing the Assembly

The hearing of the word of God proclaimed must be well prepared in the souls of the faithful by an apt knowledge of Scripture and, where pastorally possible, by special initiatives designed to deepen understanding of the biblical readings, particularly those used on Sundays and holy days. If Christian individuals and families are not regularly drawing new life from the reading of the sacred text in a spirit of prayer and docility to the Church's interpretation, then it is difficult for the liturgical proclamation of the word of God alone to produce the fruit we might expect. This is the value of initiatives in parish communities which bring together during the week those who take part in the Eucharist — priest, ministers and faithful — in order to prepare the Sunday liturgy, reflecting beforehand upon the word of God which will be proclaimed. . . . Clearly, much depends on those who exercise the ministry of the word. It is their duty to prepare the reflection on the word of the Lord by prayer and study of the sacred text, so that they may then express its contents faithfully and apply them to people's concerns and to their daily lives.

Pope John Paul II, Apostolic Letter Dies Domini, *40.*

Chapter Five

Product or Spirituality: Evaluating the Preaching Process

Authentic, effective liturgical preaching is less a matter of technique than it is a matter of passion. Nonetheless, we have spent considerable time providing techniques to help a community achieve better liturgical preaching. Take the techniques and use them and adapt them, but don't forget the passion. Preaching is, first of all, a matter of the heart.

Perhaps a safeguard would be to regard the model and the method presented here less as technique and more as exercise in spiritual formation. Through seasonal and weekly meetings, in corporate and individual work, ministers rehearse a word that will beckon others to draw closer to the Holy One. Those who help to prepare the dialogue of assembly and God that is preaching are themselves going to draw closer to God; their work is not something apart from the dialogue they help to prepare. They are themselves engaged in a conversation with God.

Liturgical preaching participates in the mystery of God's self-revelation. It is both an announcement of and encounter with God's presence. Broadly speaking, that is what our church considers a sacramental act. And if preaching itself is sacramental, isn't the preparation going to have something of a sacramental character? That preparation process itself provides the participants a way to enter more deeply into the mystery of God's self-revelation.

Many aspects of the process of preaching underscore its spiritually formative — even sacramental — character. Three of these deserve consideration.

Collaboration   Each step in the method requires working together. And we have called preaching itself a conversation, a dialogue between God and an assembly. This collaborative undertaking announces that, for Christians, union with God is not achieved apart from the community. Catholic spirituality is particularly ecclesial. This

process both flows out of such a Catholic understanding and will take it in new directions.

Journey   The Rite of Christian Initiation of Adults signals that Christian life is a journey. Christianity is not so much knowledge to be mastered as it is a pilgrimage to be undertaken. In the vision of preaching that emerges from the model and the method of this book, the ministry of preaching is anything but "product driven." The goal is not as simple as composing and delivering a great sermon. Rather, preaching is an act of accompaniment: attending to a Christian community through a process of preparation, preaching and critique in our common journey toward God. Even the end of the journey is dialogue.

Encounter   Authentic liturgical preaching as well as the model and method designed to achieve it are encounters. They are encounters with texts and rituals, current events and the arts. But most of all, the preparation and the preaching are both meant to enable that awesome encounter between people and God. This is the hope of every authentic Christian spirituality: to encounter the Holy One through a sustained and transformative dialogue.

Evaluation

Many questions are possible in evaluating liturgical preaching. Was it vibrant and engaging? Was it prophetic and challenging? Was it coherent to its liturgical context?

These are important, but they tend to focus on a single homily rather than on the ongoing process of preparation and preaching. They might not get to the heart of the matter.

A better starting point for evaluating liturgical preaching is this: Let preachers and their communities consider to what extent — over the long haul — did the collaboration in preparation and preaching express and create a new sense of church? To what extent did the preaching and the preparation engage the community more deeply and authentically in the Christian journey? To what extent did the preparation and the preaching allow this pilgrim people to encounter, to confront even, the Holy One in new and transformative ways?

Admittedly these are large and hard-to-answer questions. They should not substitute for week-by-week evaluation. Nor should they substitute for even more basic questions; for instance, could the preacher be heard clearly? But neither should they be thought of as a luxury. A year after beginning to use something based on the model and method of this book, the preachers and their collaborators should not be afraid to ponder such questions.

Saint Augustine had a relatively simple definition of sacrament. He called it "the visible word." In that phrase the famous preacher from Africa provides Christian preachers not only with a definition, but also with a fundamental goal for their preaching: to render the word tangible and visible in the life of a faith community. It is my hope and prayer that the materials presented here contribute to that noble and critical task in your community.

exercise 1: The Conversion to Method

You have a method for preparing to preach. Outline it here, including the variable things you sometimes do. Try to make explicit what may be only implicit. You may wish to think of this as handing on your own recipe.

First list the ingredients. Think of these as your own conversation partners (which may differ greatly from those discussed in Chapter 3).

1. ....

2. ....

3. ....

4. ....

5. ....

etc. ....

Then write your recipe, noting the approximate time given to each step.   *time*

1. ....

2. ....

3. ....

4. ....

5. ....

What works in this recipe?

1. ....

2. ....

3. ....

4. ....

5. ....

What does not work in this recipe?

1. ....

2. ....

3. ....

4. ....

5. ....

exercise 2: The Conversion to Collaboration

Make a list of all the ways in which your homily preparation is now collaborative. Think concretely about recent homilies as you do this.

1. ....

2. ....

3. ....

List ten people from the parish who would likely make a good contribution in a discussion of the homilies for a season.

1. ....

2. ....

3. ....

4. ....

5. ....

6. ....

7. ....

8. ....

9. ....

10. ....

Is your list balanced?
❏ *men* ❏ *women* ❏ *young* ❏ *middled-aged* ❏ *old*

What other balances would be important in your parish? (You are seeking wisdom and fruitful discussion, not simply a mix of people.)

Think about what will be said in the invitation. What are the three things you most want people to realize?

What should people do beforehand?

Where will you meet and what will make this a welcoming environment?

exercise 3: The Remote Preparation Meeting

Using Chapter 4, make a realistic agenda for the remote preparation meeting: the order of the meeting, the questions you want to raise, the length of time on each part of the meeting.

agenda item	*question*	*length*

This is a homework sheet for the next meeting. What needs to be done, who is going to do it, what is the hoped-for goal?

task	*person responsible*	*goal*

DATE OF MEETING: _____   **SUNDAYS TO BE DISCUSSED:** _____

exercise **4**: The Remote Preparation Meeting:
Individual Preparation

Fill in some or all of this grid with images, words or phrases.

Sunday	Reading I	Psalm	Reading II	Gospel	Posture/Gesture	Sacramentary

Special Rituals	Melodies & Sung Texts	Environment	Special People/Groups	Other		

DATE OF MEETING: _____   SUNDAYS TO BE DISCUSSED: _____

exercise **5**: The Human Story

1. List three parish events or issues over the last few months that have had an impact on parish life.

2. Can you name two or three concerns confronting some of the households in the parish today?

3. Who are some of the people who have joined or left your community? Why?

4. Will there be an unusual number of weddings, baptisms, anniversaries or other special events during the season under consideration? What are they?

5. Are there any stories, experiences or relationships that give you some insight into what the community needs to hear in the coming season?

DATE OF MEETING: _____   **SUNDAYS TO BE DISCUSSED:** _____

exercise 6: Group Brainstorming during the Remote Preparation Meeting

❏ Read aloud a few key passages from the scriptures from the season under consideration.

❏ Also read a few of the orations, prefaces, or music texts.

❏ Let someone different read each of these.

❏ Ask each person in the group what struck, surprised or troubled them about any single text they heard. Use this diagram to record the responses.

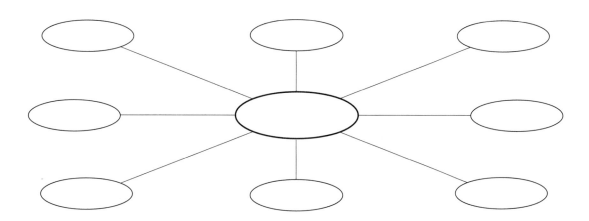

Then have people read aloud any key images or ideas from their preparation worksheets which have not yet been mentioned.

Where do the images collide? Where do they coalesce? Do some images seem stronger than others?

If you could save only five phrases or images for the whole season, which ones would they be?

DATE OF MEETING: _____   **SUNDAYS TO BE DISCUSSED:** _____

exercise **7** : World Events

In the weeks before the remote preparation meeting, make notes below in response to the questions given. At the meeting, responses will be shared aloud without explanations.

What were the major national/international news stories?

What other stories should we pay attention to? Aside from the big stories, were there troubling or important smaller news items that got your attention? Attach clippings if that helps.

What were the major local stories?

In at least one area, note the deeper movements behind the headlines. If you have found an article or some other source that was particularly helpful, bring a copy or make note of that here.

exercise 8: Intermediate Preparation

Using the text (see page 26ff), make an agenda for the second meeting. Be sure this agenda makes use of the work people did between the meetings. Be clear about the goals of this second meeting. Note the amount of time to be given to each item. Be clear about where the work will go after this meeting.

agenda item	*question*	*length*
....	....	....
....	....	....
....	....	....
....	....	....

The following areas of resolution may emerge from this meeting:

1. General direction for the season

2. Sunday to Sunday progression

3. Resources for preachers

DATE OF MEETING: _____   **SUNDAYS TO BE DISCUSSED:** _____

exercise 9: Evaluation

Take ten minutes to evaluate the last season's preaching.

Ways the plan was carried out and was effective:

Comments on how individual preachers worked with the plan:

Ways the focus or direction was accessible and helpful to the community:

What could be learned, repeated or changed in view of the strengths and weaknesses of the previous plan?

DATE OF MEETING: _____   **SUNDAYS TO BE DISCUSSED:** _____

exercise 10: Immediate Preparation Checklist

Use this exercise as a guide for your weekly homily preparation.

DATE AND NAME OF SUNDAY: _____

MONDAY

❏ Review the notes from the preparation meetings.

❏ Read out loud the lectionary and sacramentary texts for next Sunday.

❏ Look over the texts and sing some of the music for next Sunday.

Any interesting convergence of these elements?

TUESDAY

❏ Read the texts from a different English translation than that in the lectionary.

❏ Look up at least one word or concept in a biblical/theological dictionary.

Points that need to be remembered or explored from this exercise:

WEDNESDAY

▪ Guiding images for the homily:

▪ Illustrations, human stories, literature, world events to weave into the homily:

▪ Where is the best place to begin? How do I start the homily:

▪ Rough outline of the homily:

What did I leave out?

❏ Lectionary?

❏ Liturgical bible?

❏ World events?

❏ The arts?

❏ The human story?

(over)

THURSDAY

Any problems with yesterday's outline, illustrations, beginning?

Any new ideas, solutions, different starting point, rethinking of the focus?

Can I summarize the basic content and direction of the homily in a sentence or two?

FRIDAY

TIME TO WRITE A COMPLETE TEXT OR OUTLINE OF THE HOMILY.

SATURDAY

Time to practice yesterday's draft.

Does this practice suggest any changes, corrections, nuances in the text?

SUNDAY

I Am Ready!